com~~~~

Lost
for
Words

Creative messages for all occasions

Kathy Schmidt and Louise Jourdan

NEW
HOLLAND

First published in Australia in 2009 by
New Holland Publishers (Australia) Pty Ltd
Sydney • Auckland • London • Cape Town

Unit 1/66 Gibbes Street Chatswood Australia
218 Lake Road Northcoate Auckland New Zealand
Garfield House 86–88 Edgware Road London W2 2EA United Kingdom
Wembley Square First Floor Solan Road Gardens Cape Town 8001 South Africa

www.newhollandpublishers.com

A record of this book is held at the National Library of Australia

ISBN 9781741107401

Publisher: Fiona Schultz
Publishing Manager: Lliane Clarke
Project Editor: Christine Chua
Cover Design: Natasha Hayles
Production Manager: Linda Bottari
Printer: Toppan Leefung Printing Ltd (China)

Dedication
To everyone who struggles to put
pen to paper or words into cards.

Acknowledgements

We would like to thank Jeanette Fernandez—
it was your farewell party and
goodbye card which caused us to be
lost for words and hence provided the
inspiration for this series of books.
A big thank you to our husbands for
their continued encouragement.

Preface

The art of sending cards is being lost in our culture. Email, text messaging and internet chat rooms are fast becoming our main forms of communication. Despite this, or perhaps because of it, the elation on receiving a card filled with heartfelt wishes or condolences can still touch someone's heart. The recipient not only appreciates the words, but also the effort and thought that went into buying, writing and sending the card.

You may find it difficult to find a card that says what you want to say, or that exactly describes the emotions you want to share, despite the best efforts of professional greeting card writers. The choices are endless and, after browsing through the many available, you might opt for a card that is blank inside for your own verse or thoughts.

For some this might come easily, but for most of us it's a struggle to come up with the right words that best fit the occasion. Do we want to use humour or reveal deeper feelings? Do we wish to acknowledge someone's loss or success? *Lost for Words* and *Completely Lost for Words* have been written to help the hesitant card writer. Sometimes we need some inspiration to get the creative juices flowing, so use these sayings and quotes to inspire you to write something personalised and meaningful.

And while there are many occasions which call for a card to be sent—from birthdays and weddings, to the birth of a baby or a graduation—sometimes the best time to send, and receive, a card is for no particular reason.

Kathy Schmidt
Louise Jourdan

Contents

Birthdays

Birthdays are good for you. The more you have,
the longer you live.   Unknown

You deserve to be spoilt rotten on your birthday.

✳

May all your dreams come true in this special birthday year.

✳

Hoping your birthday brings with it all the things your heart holds dear.

✳

We all agree you're looking younger than ever ... Happy Birthday.

✳

It's your day—so relax and enjoy all the good things coming your way.

✳

May your Happy Birthday be perfect.

✳

What a special day, the day you came into the world.
My life has been all the better for knowing you.

✳

How would I describe (name)? In a word ... seasoned.

✳

May all the wishes you make today come true.

✳

When I see beauty, I think of you ... Happy Birthday.

✳

No-one can avoid the passing of time, so smile and enjoy every minute.

❄

You're only as old as you feel ... Happy Birthday.

❄

Fabulous, flirty and (age) ... Happy Birthday.

❄

Wishing you love, joy and laughter on your day.

❄

May your birthday be as warm and beautiful to you as you are to me.

❄

May your day be so happy that your face hurts from smiling.

❄

On your birthday, I just want to acknowledge the joy you bring to all those around you.

❄

Wish for the stars ... you deserve it.

❄

May all life's simple pleasures be yours today.

❄

Do you feel a little wiser? Happy Birthday.

❄

As the years go by we all soften a little around the edges.

❄

Embrace life and all it holds for you.

❋

May this year hold many fond memories for the future.

❋

To my dear friend who lights up the room.

❋

On the endless possibilities for the coming year ... dream big.

❋

You make all the difference in my life.

❋

No-one deserves a special day as much as you.

❋

We take pleasure in celebrating your birthday as it is a reminder of how lucky we are to have you in our life. You are a wonderful (brother/sister/daughter/friend etc).

❋

You will never go out of style.

❋

To the star of the show ... Happy Birthday.

TURNING TEN

Double figures – Wow!
Who's a big (boy/girl) now?

❋

Happy Birthday, ten-year-old ... you hardly look a day over nine.

❋

Hooray! You're turning 10 today.

❄

Congratulations. Ten years old ... and ten years wiser.

❄

Turning 10. Congratulations on reaching double figures.

❄

Happy Birthday to an amazing 10-year-old who's smart and clever with so much to offer. Keep learning and living every day.

❄

Wishing you a birthday as awesome as you are. Happy 10th Birthday.

❄

Wow! Ten years old ... a little bit taller than last year ... does that mean more cake for you and less for me?

❄

Wow! 10 years old ... getting closer to 100 every day!

❄

To a little ray of sunshine, shining brighter each year ... 10 today ... Hooray!

❄

10 today ... now the adventure begins.

THIRTEEN

It's an age of change. Don't worry, your parents are just as frightened as you are. Happy Birthday.

❄

Hey 13-year-old, getting old now ... it won't be long till you retire.

✻

Youth comes but once in a lifetime—don't grow up too fast.
Have a great day.

✻

Oh, the teenage years ... I am so excited for you!
And so afraid for your parents.

✻

Remember ... now that you're a teen, you shouldn't do anything
that wouldn't make your mother proud.

✻

Thirteen. Now, that's a reason to be excited. It's the beginning
of an amazing time of your life.

✻

So now you're 13 ... what does that mean?
Making fun of 12-year-olds, perhaps?

✻

It's your 13th birthday. May 13 wishes come true for you today.

Funky and fabulous ... you must be fourteen.
Oops, that's next year ... Happy Birthday.

✻

A 13th birthday is an event not to be missed ... thank you
for sharing your company on this special day.

✻

It's your 13th birthday ... relax, chill out and enjoy the ride.

✻

Now you are 13 you will face new challenges ... be true to yourself
and stay strong in your beliefs and you will surely succeed in
everything you do.

✻

The 13th birthday is such a special milestone ... cherish each moment and all you have achieved so far.

GIRL SIXTEEN

Sweet 16 and never been kissed ... or so you tell your parents.

❋

Sixteen is a magical time ... Enjoy every moment ... Happy 16th.

❋

You turn 16 on this day, and I'm pleased to say,
with sweetness still intact.

❋

Happy Birthday to a girl who has grown into a level-headed young woman. Your maturity and confidence at 16 have impressed us.

❋

When you came into our lives 16 years ago, we were so blessed. May you continue to bring joy to those around you. Happy Birthday.

❋

You're finally turning 16. What a great time to celebrate.

❋

Enjoy being 16. It's that glorious time of feeling grown up but without the burden of big responsibilities.

❋

Happy Birthday to the sweet 16. So young and beautiful, nothing compares to how special you are.

❋

Beautiful 16-year-old, be strong in yourself and let your beauty shine from within.

❊

To a true beauty ... Happy Sweet 16th.

❊

Happy 16th Birthday ... may every day be a good hair day.

❊

To my style queen ... happy 16th.

❊

Say goodbye to dolls and toys. Say hello to make-up and boys!
Unknown

❊

To a special 16-year-old, whatever dreams you hold, may the future bring them to you.

BOY SIXTEEN

Happy 16th ... Not long till that motorbike license ... Parents beware!

❊

To a 16-year-old legend ... Happy Birthday.

❊

Just remember ... 16, not 18. Take it easy and enjoy your day.

❊

Happy 16th. Enjoy the year ... one of the best of your life.

❊

Sweet sixteen! Sweet sixteen!
We can't believe it's true;
The person sitting before us
Is really, really you.

Sweet sixteen! Sweet sixteen!
Coloured candles on a cake!
We send you a Happy Birthday
With a wish for you to make!
Shirley J. Davidson

Reaching 16 is a milestone,
a happy point in life.
You've set your personality.
and your tolerance for strife.

By now you know right from wrong
and how to influence friends.
It's time to look down the road
at forks and around the bends.

The road ahead is wonderful,
some choices will be clear.
Your path depends on bravery
to push aside the fear.

When you chose this way or that,
slow choices or if snappy,
make the choices best for you,
the ones that make you happy.
Unknown

EIGHTEEN

18? Congratulations! Now you can finally say
'Stop treating me like a kid'.

✳

Now that you're 18 society feels you are mature enough to vote.
The first thing to vote for is an all-night party to celebrate.

✳

Now that you're 18 freedom is yours ... what are you waiting for?
Happy Birthday.

✳

Turning 18, what does that really mean? It means you can vote, drink
and be tried as an adult in court. What, not as exciting
as you thought?! Have a great day.

✳

You're not just 18 today—you're all the ages you've ever been.
So now that you're an adult, don't forget the kid inside.

✳

Now that you're 18 the world is your oyster ... what's first
on the agenda?

✳

Registering to vote?
Joining the army?
Moving out of home?
Or just having a massive party? ... Happy Birthday

✳

Happy 18th birthday. May this year, your first officially
as an adult, be simply amazing.

❊

Common sense is the collection of prejudices acquired by age 18.
Albert Einstein

❊

I cried on my 18th birthday. I thought 17 was such a nice age.
You're young enough to get away with things,
but you're old enough, too. Liv Tyler

TWENTY-ONE

• •

21 ... Congratulations—the beginning of a new phase in your life.
Make it an exciting one.

❊

You make this world a better place, you deserve this special day. Lots
of love on your 21st birthday.

❊

Happy 21st. Looking forward to watching all your dreams come true.

❊

At 21, you feel like you can take on the world. Have fun trying.

❊

Congratulations on turning 21. May doors open to
new and wonderful opportunities.

❊

There is a special name for people who stay home on their birthday ...
LOSER ... Hope you have a great night out on your 21st birthday.

❊

Happy 21st birthday ... this is just the start of amazing things to come.

✳

Here's to you on your 21st birthday. Have a good one!

✳

May this day be as warm and wonderful as you are ... Happy 21st.

✳

So now you are 21 ... growing up is still optional! Happy Birthday.

✳

We are so happy to be able to celebrate this special day and all the achievements you have made along the way ... Happy 21st!

FOR TEENS/THE YOUNG

One of the advantages of being young is that you don't let common sense get in the way of doing things everyone else knows are impossible. Unknown

✳

Today, be aware of how you are spending your 1440 beautiful moments, and spend them wisely. Unknown

✳

No man is ever old enough to know better. Holbrook Jackson

✳

The longer I live the more beautiful life becomes. Frank Lloyd Wright

✳

The surprising thing about young fools is how many survive to become old fools. Doug Larson

✳

Unless you try to do something beyond what you have already mastered, you will never grow. Ronald E Osborn

❋

Start by doing what's necessary; then do what's possible; and suddenly you are doing the impossible.   St Francis of Assisi

❋

Remember, if you ever need a helping hand, you'll find one at the end of your arm ... As you grow older you will discover that you have two hands. One for helping yourself, the other for helping others. Audrey Hepburn

❋

Success does not come to those who wait ... and it does not wait for anyone to come to it. Unknown

❋

Start where you are. Distant fields always look greener, but opportunity lies right where you are. Take advantage of every opportunity of service. Robert Collier

❋

Start every day with an inspiring thought. Unknown

❋

The real secret of success is enthusiasm.   Walter Chrysler

❋

Remember that as a teenager you are in the last stage of your life when you will be happy to hear the phone is for you. Fran Leibowitz

❋

The best way to keep children at home is to make the home atmosphere pleasant, and let the air out of the tyres.
Dorothy Parker

❋

You can only be young once. But you can always be immature.
Dave Barry

✳

When buying a used car, punch the buttons on the radio. If all the stations are rock and roll, there's a good chance the transmission is shot. Larry Lujack

✳

The invention of the teenager was a mistake. Once you identify a period of life in which people get to stay out late but don't have to pay taxes—naturally, no-one wants to live any other way.
Judith Martin

✳

Mothers of teenagers know why animals eat their young.
Unknown

30TH BIRTHDAY

When you turn 30, a whole new thing happens: you see yourself acting like your parents. Blair Sabol

✳

After 30, a body has a mind of its own. Bette Midler

✳

A man 30 years old, I said to myself, should have his field of life all ploughed, and his planting well done; for after that it is summer time. Lew Wallace

40TH BIRTHDAY

Be wise with speed; a fool at 40 is a fool indeed.
Edward Young

Every man over 40 is a scoundrel.   George Bernard Shaw

✳

You're not 40, you're 18 with 22 years' experience.   Unknown

✳

*What most persons consider as virtue after the age of 40
is simply a loss of energy.*   Voltaire

✳

The best years of a woman's life—the ten years between 39 and 40.
Unknown

✳

*Life begins at 40—but so do fallen arches, rheumatism, faulty
eyesight, and the tendency to tell a story to the same person,
three or four times.*   Helen Rowland

✳

*At the age of 20, we don't care what the world thinks of us; at 30,
we worry about what it is thinking of us; at 40, we discover that it
wasn't thinking of us at all.*   Unknown

✳

*The 'I just woke up' face of your thirties is
the 'all day long' face of your forties.*   Libby Reid

OLDER BIRTHDAY

Looking 50 is great—if you're 60.   Joan Rivers

✳

*The man who views the world at 50 the same as he did at 20 has
wasted 30 years of his life.*   Muhammad Ali

I think when the full horror of being 50 hits you, you should stay home and have a good cry. Alan Bleasdale

❋

Forty is the old age of youth; 50 is the youth of old age. Unknown

❋

I'm aiming by the time I'm 50 to stop being an adolescent.
Wendy Cope

❋

Some people reach the age of 60 before others. Lord Hood

❋

I have achieved my 70 years in the usual way, by sticking strictly to a scheme of life which would kill anybody else ... I will offer here, as a sound maxim, this: That we can't reach old age by another man's road.
Mark Twain, at his 70th birthday dinner

❋

One starts to get young at the age of 60 and then it is too late.
Pablo Picasso

❋

If I had to live again I would do exactly the same thing. Of course I have regrets, but if you are 60 years old and you have no regrets then you haven't lived. Christy Moore

❋

Oh to be 70 again.
Georges Clemenceau

Age is not measured by years. Nature does not equally distribute energy. Some people are born old and tired while others are going strong at 70. Dorothy Thompson

❋

By the time you're 80 years old you've learned everything. You only have to remember it. George Burns

❋

A man of 80 has outlived probably three new schools of painting, two of architecture and poetry and a hundred in dress.
Joyce Carey

MIDDLE AGE

Middle age is when a guy keeps turning off lights for economical rather than romantic reasons. Eli Cass

❋

Middle age is when work is a lot less fun and fun is a lot more work. Unknown

❋

Middle age is when your age starts to show around your middle.
Bob Hope

❋

Probably the happiest period in life most frequently is in middle age, when the eager passions of youth are cooled, and the infirmities of age not yet begun; as we see that the shadows, which are at morning and evening so large, almost entirely disappear at midday. Thomas Arnold

❋

The only time you really live fully is from 30 to 60. The young are slaves to dreams; the old servants of regrets. Only the middle-aged have all their five senses in the keeping of their wits. Hervey Allen

❋

Middle age is the awkward period when Father Time catches up with Mother Nature. Harold Coffin

OLD AGE

We know we're getting old when the only thing we want for our birthday is not to be reminded of it. Unknown

❈

I still have a full deck; I just shuffle slower now. Unknown

❈

Old age is like everything else. To make a success of it, you've got to start young. Fred Astaire

❈

Therefore we do not lose heart. Even though our outward man is perishing, yet the inward man is being renewed day by day.
The Bible, 2 Corinthians 4:16

❈

To resist the frigidity of old age, one must combine the body, the mind, and the heart. And to keep these in parallel vigour one must exercise, study, and love. Bonstettin

❈

By the time you find greener pastures, you can't climb the fence!
Unknown

❈

You don't stop laughing because you grow old. You grow old because you stop laughing. Michael Pritchard

❈

Growing old is inevitable ... growing up is optional. Unknown

❈

You are never too old to set another goal or to dream a new dream.
Les Brown

❈

To keep the heart unwrinkled, to be hopeful, kindly, cheerful, reverent, that is to triumph over old age. Thomas B Aldrich

❋

I'm at an age when my back goes out more than I do. Phyllis Diller

❋

You're never too old to become younger. Mae West

❋

Just remember, once you're over the hill you begin to pick up speed. Charles Schulz

❋

In case you're worried about what is going to become of the younger generation, it's going to grow up and start worrying about the younger generation. Roger Allen

❋

Youth is a circumstance you can't do anything about. The trick is to grow up without getting old. Frank Lloyd Wright

❋

It is not all bad, this getting old, ripening. After the fruit has got its growth it should juice up and mellow. God forbid I should live long enough to ferment and rot and fall to the ground in a squash.
Emily Carr

❋

Age is a high price to pay for maturity. Tom Stoppard

❋

They say that age is all in your mind. The trick is keeping it from creeping down into your body. Unknown

❋

Growing old is like being increasing penalised for a crime you have not committed. Anthony Powell

❋

Lying about my age is easier now, since I sometimes forget what it is. Unknown

❋

No wise man ever wished to be younger. Jonathan Swift

❋

In youth we run into difficulties. In old age difficulties run into us. Josh Billings

❋

You know you are getting old when the candles cost more than the cake. Bob Hope

❋

I'm very pleased with each advancing year. It stems back to when I was 40. I was a bit upset about reaching that milestone, but an older friend consoled me. 'Don't complain about growing old—many, many people do not have that privilege.' Earl Warren

❋

Wisdom doesn't automatically come with old age. Nothing does—except wrinkles. It's true, some wines improve with age. But only if the grapes were good in the first place. Abigail Van Buren

MORE BIRTHDAYS

The best birthdays of all are those that haven't arrived yet. Robert Orben

❋

Wisdom doesn't necessarily come with age. Sometimes age just shows up all by itself. Tom Wilson

❋

The old believe everything; the middle-aged suspect everything; the young know everything. Oscar Wilde

✳

When I was younger, I could remember anything, whether it happened or not. Mark Twain

✳

Few women admit their age. Few men act theirs.   Unknown

✳

Time may be a great healer, but it's a lousy beautician.   Unknown

✳

What could be more beautiful than a dear old lady growing wise with age? Every age can be enchanting, provided you live within it. Brigitte Bardot

✳

The older I grow the more I distrust the familiar doctrine that age brings wisdom.   H J Mencken

✳

Count your life by smiles, not tears. Count your age by friends, not years.   Unknown

The secret of staying young is to live honestly, eat slowly, and lie about your age.   Lucille Ball

✳

The best way to remember your wife's birthday is to forget it once. H V Prochnow

✳

I never forget my wife's birthday. It's usually the day after she reminds me about it.   Unknown

✳

A well adjusted woman is one who not only knows what she wants for her birthday, but even knows what she's going to exchange it for.   Unknown

Valentine

The most beautiful view is the one I share with you. Unknown

✻

You are the only one I wish to spend this day with.
Thank you for being my Valentine.

✻

You caught my eye, then captured my heart.

✻

To me you are love personified. I hear love in your voice,
see love in your eyes and feel love in your touch.
Thank you for the beauty of your love each day.

✻

I have never known a love so strong, so secure; a place for us
to dwell side by side from here to eternity.

✻

To my Valentine, I need to take this moment to let you know how
much I value our love and how much it means to have you in my life.
Words cannot express the happiness you bring into my life each day.

✻

To the sweetest thing in the world ... I love you sweetie pie.

✻

I long to call you mine, sweet Valentine.

✻

I have not been feeling myself lately. I am weak at the knees, my
brain is like mush, I cannot sleep at night, my heart is racing and my
stomach is doing flips and it's all because of you
and the wonderful way you make me feel inside.

To the love of my life—may your day be filled with love, laughter and smiles. Love and kisses ...

✻

I love the words you say, the things you do and the way you show the love we share in our lives each day.

✻

Two hearts beating together no matter how adverse the weather.

✻

The love in your smile makes me feel that all is possible. I love you.

✻

Although we are apart and the days are so long, I will never stop counting the days till we can be together and at last forever.

✻

From the moment we met our spirits united, from the moment we met my heart was in love with you. From the moment we met I wanted to share my life with you. I love you.

✻

If we had never met, where would I be? Searching the world far and wide till I had you by my side.

✻

When the sun has set and the day is done, come home to me and let's have some fun!

✻

Your love shines so bright in my life that it makes all my woes disappear.

✻

Love isn't always easy, but you're worth it. I'll love you always.

❋

'You and me' is everything to me ... It's all I dream to ever be ...
Thanks for the love you give to me.

❋

I've been thinking of you today.

❋

When I feel life gets too hard and I feel broken inside, you have
always been the only one who could put me back together.

❋

It took so long for us to find each other. So long for you to
walk into my life. Now that you are here, I will hold onto you forever.
I need you in my life.

❋

All I have I give to you ... this is me, my heart, my love,
I give it all to you. I love you.

❋

Our lives together have been a wonderful adventure. Ups and downs,
twists and turns. I wouldn't have it any other way.

❋

Thank you for believing in me and my hopes and dreams for the future.
Please be with me every step of the way.

❋

Across the miles I send you smiles and
on the wings of a dove I send you love.

❋

I believe in you and the love we share. I believe it will
last a lifetime through the good times and the hard times.
I believe we can stand the test of time.

❋

My heart chose you, and I wouldn't have it any other way.

✻

As the stars in the sky, the sand on the beach, the drops
in the ocean are endless, so is this love of ours.

✻

When I hear music ... I think of you
When I hear laughter ... I think of you
When I feel warmth ... I think of you ...
because you are the most beautiful thing in my life.

✻

It is a miracle that we found each other. A gift from God ...
from me to you and you to me.

✻

I feel blessed as blessed can be ... simply because you want me.

✻

You catch me when I fall and pick me up when I am down.

✻

You make me feel like sunshine.

✻

Somebody loves you ... somebody needs you ... all my love
from the bottom of my heart.

✻

What would I do without you? 'Cause love is me and you.

✻

Even when we are not together, you are always with me,
safe in the love that encompasses us.

✻

Even though we are far apart, our love stretches from heart to heart.

❊

I store the memories of the love we share deep in my heart
and seal it with a kiss.

❊

Gravitation is not responsible for people falling in love.
Albert Einstein

❊

A hundred hearts would be too few. To carry all my love for you.
Unknown

❊

*Oh, if it be to choose and call thee mine, love, thou art every day
my Valentine!* Thomas Hood

❊

*Anyone can catch your eye, but it takes someone special
to catch your heart.* Unknown

Engagement

*Love one another and you will be happy.
It's as simple and as difficult as that.*
Michael Leunig

❊

May your engagement be the beginning of a fairytale that
ends with 'Happily Ever After'.

❊

You're a match made in heaven. Congratulations.

❊

When things start to get crazy as you prepare for your wedding day, look back and remember the love you shared on this engagement day.

✳

To a very special couple ... you make a perfect pair.

✳

It's no surprise ... you were made for each other. Congratulations.

✳

We hope that all your dreams come true and wish for your future happiness and days filled with joy.

✳

Love is the expansion of two natures in such fashion that each include the other, each is enriched by the other. Felix Adler

✳

An engaged woman is always more agreeable than a disengaged. She is satisfied with herself. Her cares are over, and she feels that she may exert all her powers of pleasing without suspicion. All is safe with a lady engaged; no harm can be done. Jane Austen

✳

The person who tries to live alone will not succeed as a human being. His heart withers if it does not answer another heart. His mind shrinks away if he hears only the echoes of his own thoughts and finds no other inspiration. Pearl S Buck

✳

My mother says I didn't open my eyes for eight days after I was born, but when I did, the first thing I saw was an engagement ring. I was hooked. Elizabeth Taylor

✳

When you realise you want to spend the rest of your life with somebody, you want the rest of your life to start as soon as possible. Harry in the film *When Harry Met Sally*

Engagement

Long engagements give people the opportunity of finding out each other's character before marriage, which is never advisable.
Oscar Wilde

Love is friendship set on fire.   Jeremy Taylor

*Love is a miracle, sweet as can be,
That will always remain a complete mystery.
For though it is something that's centuries old,
It cannot be purchased for silver or gold.
But instead must be given of one's own free will,
And received with no promises it must fulfil.
And once it's exchanged in this time-honoured way,
There's nothing that love cannot manage to say.
No problem's too great and no problem's too small,
For love, like a miracle, conquers them all.
And leaves in their place such a feeling of peace,
That joy, just like love, cannot help but increase!*
Unknown

*As you start out together
Along life's busy road
Remember, bring your dreams with you,
They lighten every load.
And then you will discover
As your journey starts today
That happiness walks with you
Hand-in-hand along the way.*
Unknown

Kitchen Tea

The Kitchen: Where food, fun, love and laughter and wild plans come together. Unknown

✲

May the many hours you spend in your kitchen be filled with love, laughter and eating.

✲

Wishing you both many happy memories of cooking triumphs and disasters as you spend time together in the heart of the home.

✲

Praying that the times you share in the kitchen are an adventure and not a chore.

✲

Season your kitchen with love.

✲

Hoping you discover more about each other as you spend time together in the kitchen, cooking, eating and cleaning up.

✲

Enjoy your time in the kitchen together. Remember to love and cook with wild abandon.

✲

One of the delights of life is eating with friends, second to that is talking about eating. And, for an unsurpassed double whammy, there is talking about eating while you are eating with friends. Laurie Colwin in her book *Home Cooking*

*There is no spectacle on earth more appealing than that of a
beautiful woman in the act of cooking dinner
for someone she loves.* Thomas Wolfe

*We may live without friends; we may live without books, but
civilised men cannot live without cooks.* Edward G Bulweri Lytton

*In the childhood memories of every good cook, there's a large
kitchen, a warm stove, a simmering pot and a Mum.*
Barbara Costikyan

*There is one thing more exasperating than a spouse who can cook
and won't, and that's a spouse who can't cook and will.* Unknown

*Kitchen Rules: There's no such things as girl's work or boy's work—
there's just work and it has to get done.* Unknown

Marriage

*The goal of marriage is not to think alike,
but to think together.* Unknown

Congratulations. We know this is the beginning
of a wonderful success story.

Don't forget your individuality as you unite together as one, those
qualities that make each of you special and are why you fell in love.

Love each other, talk to each other but most of all forgive each other; then the journey will be sweet.

✻

We couldn't have asked for a better way to spend our day—being witness to the beginning of a great love story. Congratulations.

✻

We are so glad we are able to share this special day with you. You are the perfect couple and we know this is just the beginning of a beautiful journey as you travel life's road together.

✻

We know the build-up to the ceremony can be exhausting, so here's hoping you survived ... have a wonderful day and a fantastic honeymoon. Enjoy each other.

✻

Wishing you all that love and life together has to offer ... as the years progress, may your love and the joys you experience deepen.

✻

We are so happy to celebrate your transition from best friends to soul mates ... Wishing you a beautiful future full of love, laughter and prosperity.

✻

May this day bring to you all your dreams and all the gifts on your bridal registry!

✻

As you embark on this new journey together, may your path be filled with new beginnings leading to a fulfilling future.

✻

A match made in heaven ... We know your dreams will all come true ... Congratulations.

✻

A successful marriage requires falling in love many times, always with the same person. Mignon McLaughlin

✳

The best is yet to be. Robert Browning

✳

You don't marry someone you can live with—you marry the person you cannot live without. Unknown

✳

The success of marriage comes not in finding the 'right' person, but in the ability of both partners to adjust to the real person they inevitably realise they married. John Fischer

✳

It is sometimes essential for a husband and wife to quarrel—they get to know each other better. Goethe

✳

Ultimately the bond of all companionship, whether in marriage or in friendship, is conversation. Oscar Wilde

✳

The first duty of love is to listen. Paul Tillich

✳

As for the secret to staying married: My wife tells me that if I ever decide to leave, she is coming with me. Jon Bon Jovi

✳

There is nothing more admirable than two people who see eye-to-eye keeping house as man and wife, confounding their enemies, and delighting their friends. Homer, 9th century BC

✳

A married man should forget his mistakes; no use two people remembering the same thing. Duane Dewel

Anniversary

Love is something eternal; the aspect may change, but not the essence. Vincent Van Gogh

FROM HUSBAND OR WIFE

I was lucky to find my true love and best friend when I met you. Thank you for every year we have been together. Each year I fall more in love with you ... Happy Anniversary.

❋

How did I get so lucky? It must have been fate, to win the heart of my soul mate.

❋

To my love bird ... what a pair we make.

❋

Still in love after all this time ... who would have thought? I didn't think, I knew, because I've always loved you.

❋

May our special journey together never end ... from here to eternity, all my love.

❋

As the years go by the sweet memories accumulate. Not one will ever be forgotten. Happy Anniversary my love.

❋

As we have shared and given over the years, my love has grown deeper.

❋

The foundation of our love is so stable ... we were built to last.

✳

May the happiness we share today be ours tomorrow and forever.

✳

Ours is a match made in heaven ... Happy Anniversary.

✳

To my love everlasting. Happy Anniversary.

✳

The honeymoon continues.

TO ANOTHER COUPLE ON THEIR ANNIVERSARY

When I look at you together, I think if only everyone
could be so lucky. Happy Anniversary.

✳

To a very special couple ... May this year be the happiest yet ...
Warm wishes.

✳

No-one is that good at acting—it must be the real thing.
Your love for each other grows and it shows. Happy Anniversary.

✳

Today we celebrate the love that was destined to be: the love of (name)
and (name). Best wishes for your eternal future together.

✳

May your love continue to flourish as you grow together.
You are both so special to us. Happy Anniversary.

✿

When a marriage radiates love like yours,
you know you are truly blessed.

✿

They say that after years together couples start to look alike ... so true.
To a handsome couple ... Happy Anniversary.

✿

Still in love after all this time. Congratulations on your everlasting love.

✿

To Mum and Dad. You have taught (us/me) so much about
relationships through your daily displays of patience, understanding,
communication and sacrifice. Happy Anniversary.

✿

*Coming together is the beginning. Keeping together is progress.
Working together is success.* Henry Ford

✿

*The development of a really good marriage is not a natural process.
It is an achievement.* David and Vera Mace

New Baby

A baby is born with a need to be loved—and never outgrows it.
Frank A Clark

✿

It doesn't matter what they say: your life is about to change ...
for the better. Congratulations.

❋

Glad to hear there is a beautiful new face to light up the world.

❋

So happy to hear that (baby's name) arrived safe and sound. Congratulations.

❋

Dear (baby's name), you have the best parents in the world. I look forward to seeing you grow into the amazing person you are destined to be.

❋

The cutest fingers, the cutest toes, the sweetest lips and button nose.

❋

Just remember ... the overwhelming tiredness fades when you hear those first coos, see that first smile and feel those tiny fingers wrapped around yours. Congratulations, it's all worth it.

❋

Congratulations on your new precious gift, a life to nurture.

❋

May the ensuing months be filled with sweet and uninterrupted dreams for the whole family.

❋

How amazing is this new love you feel for this beautiful gift from God ... Congratulations.

❋

As your heart fills with love, may your days fill with happiness.

❋

May you savour the miracle of this new life entrusted to you. You will both be wonderful parents.

✽

A star is born that will light up your lives.

✽

Enjoy every minute they are awake, but when they go to sleep ...
YOU need to sleep.

✽

Soon you will see a smile that will forever melt your heart.

✽

Welcome, (baby's name), into the hearts of all your family
who will always love you.

✽

Hey baby, welcome to the world.

✽

Coochee coochee coo, ga ga, goo goo. Welcome to baby talk.
Congratulations.

✽

A baby is cuddles and tickles on toes,
The sweet scent of powder, a kiss on the nose! Unknown

✽

People who say they sleep like a baby usually don't have one.
Leo J Burke

Making the decision to have a child is momentous. It is to decide
forever to have your heart go walking around outside your body.
Elizabeth Stone

✽

A new baby is like the beginning of all things—wonder, hope,
a dream of possibilities. Eda J Le Shan

✽

*Life is filled with lots of things that make it all worthwhile,
but none is better than the love found in your baby's smile.*
Unknown

✳

*A baby will make love stronger, days shorter, nights longer,
bankroll smaller, home happier, clothes shabbier, the past
forgotten, and the future worth living for.* Unknown

✳

*If one feels the need of something grand, something infinite,
something that makes one feel aware of God, one need not go far
to find it. I think that I see something deeper, more infinite, more
eternal than the ocean in the expression of the eyes of a little baby
when it wakes in the morning and coos or laughs because it sees
the sun shining on its cradle.* Vincent Van Gogh

Christening

As you christen your beautiful baby, may God's blessings continue
to flow over you as you grow together as a family.

✳

It's (name's) Christening day. On this very special day, be filled with
pride as you look at your beautiful (daughter/son).

✳

Congratulations on this special day. Remember the words
of the Lord ... 'Behold, I am with you and will keep you
wherever you go ...' *The Bible*, Genesis 28:15

✳

On this day we send our best wishes and pray for a guardian angel to
watch over (name), to protect and guide (her/him) as they grow.

❋

Congratulations on this special day. We look forward to seeing you grow into a beautiful person inside and out.

❋

We send best wishes on this day as (name) is baptised before family and friends.

❋

Congratulations ... Wishing you beauty and happiness for the rest of your life.

❋

On your Christening day, we thank God for the wonderful, special miracle you are.

❋

We are so excited to be sharing this special day with you and look forward to watching your little one fulfil (his/her) purpose.

❋

May (name) grow knowing they are loved by you and by God.

❋

We celebrate with you today as this beautiful child is raised in a family knowing God's love.

❋

Remember the words of the Lord Jesus Christ,
how he said, 'Let the children come to me,
do not hinder them; for to such belongs the kingdom of God.'
The Bible, Matthew 19:14

❋

May the Lord give His angel charge over you, to guide you in all your ways. *The Bible*, Psalm 91:11

❋

If I had influence with the good fairy who is supposed to preside over the christening of all children, I should ask that her gift to each child in the world be a sense of wonder so indestructible that it would last throughout life. Rachel Carson

❄

Lord, bless this tiny infant,
Who is brought to you today,
And teach those precious little feet,
To follow in your way.
Lord, bless the baby's parents, too,
And with your loving care,
Grant them all the happiness,
A family can share.
Unknown

❄

A precious angel from heaven above will be welcomed into God's family with love. Unknown

❄

I love these little people; and it is not a slight thing, when they, who are so fresh from God, love us. Charles Dickens

❄

Now I lay me down to sleep,
I pray Thee, Lord, Thy child to keep:
Thy love guard me through the night
And wake me with the morning light. Prayer

❄

Every child born into the world is a new thought of God.
An ever fresh and radiant possibility. Kate Douglas Wiggins

❄

In praising or loving a child, we love and praise not that which is, but that which we hope for. Goethe

Mother's Day

If at first you don't succeed, do it like your mother told you.
Unknown

❉

If only I could have experienced being a mother for a day when I was a child I would have been a lot better behaved! Thanks for the amazing patience you have always shown me.

❉

Thank you for the influence you have been on my life. I don't know where or who I would be without you.

❉

I love that I can call you anytime, night or day, and you will know exactly what to say.

❉

I have learnt so much from your loving, compassionate and beautiful nature. You are my inspiration.

❉

Mum, you give me the courage and determination to go out into the world and face my fears and find success.

❉

Now that I have children of my own, I appreciate you a whole lot more. Sorry it took such a long time.

❉

Mum, thank you for guiding me each day with love and grace, building my strength and independence.

❉

I did not always agree with the things you said or did, but without your principles and love, I would not be the person I am today. Thank you.

✳

Because of you ... I can conquer the world.

✳

Thank you for standing by me and believing in me even when I was difficult. I could always count on your support to pull me through.

✳

To the most accomplished woman I know ... I am so proud to be your (daughter/son).

✳

To the most important person in my life ...
I am proud to call you my Mum.

✳

The older I get the more I appreciate all that you are in my life.

✳

The dedication, understanding and patience you show me
will always be appreciated. Thanks for being there.

✳

Thank you for helping all my dreams come true.

✳

My mother had a great deal of trouble with me, but I think she enjoyed it. Mark Twain

✳

Being a full-time mother is one of the highest salaried jobs in my field, since the payment is pure love. Mildred B Vermont

✳

She never quite leaves her children at home, even when she doesn't take them along. Margaret Culkin Banning

The mother's heart is the child's schoolroom.   Henry Ward Beecher

✳

I love my mother as the trees love water and sunshine—she helps me grow, prosper, and reach great heights.   Adabella Radici

✳

A mother is a person who, seeing there are only four pieces of pie for five people, promptly announces she never did care for pie.
Tenneva Jordan

✳

If evolution really works, how come mothers only have two hands?
Milton Berle

✳

A suburban mother's role is to deliver children obstetrically once, and by car forever after.   Peter De Vries

✳

When you are a mother, you are never really alone in your thoughts. A mother always has to think twice, once for herself and once for her child.
Sophia Loren in her book *Women and Beauty*

✳

Mother love is the fuel that enables a normal human being to do the impossible.   Marion C Garretty, quoted in *A Little Spoonful of Chicken Soup for the Mother's Soul*

✳

Now, as always, the most automated appliance in a household is the mother.   Beverly Jones

✳

The joys of motherhood are never fully experienced until the children are in bed.   Unknown

Father's Day

He didn't tell me how to live; he lived,
and let me watch him do it. Clarence Budington Kelland

✻

Thank you for being my father. You have loved, protected
and guided me and I only hope I can be the father to my kids
that you have been to me.

✻

When I fell down, you picked me up ... When I was sad you made
me laugh ...When I was scared you comforted me ...
You're everything a Dad should be.

✻

Thinking of you on this special day and the difference
your presence has made in my life.

✻

Thanks for such a great start to life.

✻

You showed me how to live honestly, lovingly and courageously.

✻

Dad, you are always someone I will look up to no matter
how tall I grow.

✻

Thank you for being the best example of 'how to live life'
a child could ask for.

✻

Thanks for all the good times, Dad. I'm looking forward to many more.

❇

Thank you for being the one I could always count on.

❇

Your integrity sets you above the rest. I'm lucky to have such
a great role model.

❇

Will I ever be able to fill your shoes? You are such an inspiration.

❇

One word to describe my Dad ... ingenious.

❇

I never had a chance to choose the man to be my Dad,
But I thank my lucky stars for the taste my mother had. Unknown

❇

By the time a man realises that maybe his father was right, he
usually has a son who thinks he's wrong. Charles Wadworth

❇

Sometimes the poorest man leaves his children
the richest inheritance. Ruth E Renkel

❇

I love my father as the stars—he's a bright shining example
and a happy twinkling in my heart. Adabella Radici

❇

A truly rich man is one whose children run into his arms
when his hands are empty. Unknown

❇

When I was a boy of 14, my father was so ignorant I could hardly
stand to have the old man around. But when I got to be 21, I was
astonished at how much he had learned in 7 years.
Mark Twain in his memoir, *Old Times on the Mississippi*

✳

I talk and talk and talk, and I haven't taught people in 50 years what my father taught by example in one week. Mario Cuomo

✳

*My father used to play with my brother and me in the yard. Mother would come out and say, 'You're tearing up the grass.'
'We're not raising grass,' Dad would reply. 'We're raising boys.'*
Harmon Killebrew

✳

*Fatherhood is pretending the present you love most
is soap-on-a-rope.* Bill Cosby

✳

Father! To God himself we cannot give a holier name.
William Wordsworth

✳

A father carries pictures where his money used to be. Unknown

✳

*Small boys become big men through the influence of big men
who care about small boys.* Unknown

✳

*The greatest gift I ever had
Came from God; I call him Dad!* Unknown

✳

*I cannot think of any need in childhood as strong as the need
for a father's protection.* Sigmund Freud

✳

*There's something like a line of gold thread running through a
man's words when he talks to his daughter, and gradually over the
years it gets to be long enough for you to pick up in your hands
and weave into a cloth that feels like love itself.*
John Gregory Brown in his book *Decorations in a Ruined Cemetery*

Friendship

Friends are the family we choose ourselves. Unknown

✳

Thank you for being a true friend. You have overlooked
my weaknesses and encouraged me in my strengths.
Thank you for accepting me just as I am.

✳

Oh, how much fun we have had over the years.
So much love, laughter and many memories.

✳

Thank you for being there through times of laughter, smiling, crying
and sighing ... Looking forward to many more happy times together.

✳

A friendship like ours is as rare as diamonds.

✳

You are always there with your pearls of wisdom ... Thank you.

✳

I know you're a true friend because you tell me how it is—everyone else
tells me what I want to hear. Thanks for keeping it honest.

✳

Trouble? Us? Never!

✳

Thank you for sharing your strength with me over this difficult time.

✳

You make my world a happier place.

✳

I feel blessed to have you as a friend. There is no need for pretence—
you allow me to be just as I am.

✳

Thanks for being there in the good and the bad times.
Your friendship means the world to me.

✳

May the sun never set on our friendship.

✳

You have helped my dreams come true ... I hope I can do
the same for you.

✳

To my partner in crime ... Thanks for all the fun we have had.

✳

To my cool, smart, happy-go-lucky, beautiful friend ... I just had to let
you know how much our friendship means to me. I love you.

✳

Dear (name) ... Thanks for always sharing.

✳

Our friendship ... magic!

✳

A friend is a companion of affection and esteem.
Thank you for being mine.

✳

To my fellow life traveller ... let's stick to the same path.

✳

Our friendship is irreplaceable.

✳

To my soul sister, may our exceptional friendship
last from here to eternity.

✳

You are the only one who understands me when I make no sense at all.

✳

Even though we are far apart, I don't know what I would do
without our conversations. Let's talk again soon.

✳

Even though life is busy just now, I am still thinking of you
and the value of our friendship.

✳

Our friendship is more beautiful to me than a bouquet of roses.

✳

Your friendship has been a ray of sunshine in my life.

✳

You have made all the difference in my life.

✳

I can live without a lot of things ... You're not one of them.

✳

You are my greatest friend, the one I can share my true feelings with.
Thank you.

✳

Every day is brighter from knowing you. You are a true friend.

✳

*Life is partly what we make it, and partly what it is made by the
friends we choose.* Tennessee Williams

❋

You meet people who forget you. You forget people you meet. But sometimes you meet those people you can't forget. Those are your friends. Unknown

❋

Real friends are those who, when you feel you've made a fool of yourself, don't feel you've done a permanent job. Unknown

❋

Friendship is always a sweet responsibility, never an opportunity. Kahlil Gibran

❋

True friendship isn't about being there when it's convenient; it's about being there when it's not. Unknown

❋

A friend is someone who knows the song in your heart and can sing it back to you when you have forgotten the words. Unknown

❋

Friends are the pillars on your porch. Sometimes they hold you up, sometimes they lean on you, and sometimes it's just enough to know that they are standing by. Unknown

❋

Celebrate the happiness that friends are always giving,
Make every day a holiday and celebrate just living!
Amanda Bradley

❋

The most beautiful discovery true friends make is that they can grow separately without growing apart. Elisabeth Foley

❋

Only your real friends tell you when your face is dirty. Sicilian proverb

Your secrets are safe with me and all my friends.   Unknown

✳

I get by with a little help from my friends.   John Lennon

✳

A true friend is someone who thinks that you are a good egg even though he knows that you are slightly cracked.   Bernard Meltzer

Thank You

*I can no other answer make,
but, thanks, and thanks.*
William Shakespeare

✳

Thank you for supporting me in my time of need.

✳

Thank you ... You made my day.

✳

Thank you. You are the key that opens doors.

✳

I am touched by all you have done ... Thank you.

✳

Thank you for all the little things you do. It means the world to me.

✳

It only takes one person's random act of kindness to make a difference. Thank you for making a difference in my life.

✳

Many thanks. May your kindness be returned to you a hundredfold.

✳

You made what was a difficult situation much easier to bear.
Thank you.

✳

Thank you for helping me get through a tough time, for your shoulder
to cry on and for listening to me blabber on and on.

✳

Your generosity and kind heart will never be forgotten. Thank you.

✳

Thank you for your grace in this situation. You are a beautiful person.

✳

While others talked, you acted. Thank you.

✳

You have moved my heart. Thank you.

✳

Thank you for giving up your precious time and energy
to make my load easier.

✳

I am touched by your love. Thank you.

✳

Thank you for being there when I needed you most.

✳

Your thoughtfulness has made such a difference in my life.

✳

Your act of kindness has touched me more than you know. Thank you.

❋

I clearly have impeccable taste in friends ... Thank you.

❋

*The smallest act of kindness is worth more
than the grandest intention.* Oscar Wilde

❋

How beautiful a day can be when kindness touches it!
George Elliston

❋

*What we have done for ourselves alone dies with us; what we have
done for others and the world remains and is immortal.* Albert Pike

❋

*Kindness is the language which the deaf can hear
and the blind can see.* Mark Twain

❋

*The only people with whom you should try to get even are those
who have helped you.* John E Southard

❋

*One can pay back the loan of gold, but one lies forever
in debt to those who are kind.* Malayan proverb

❋

*Unselfish and noble actions are the most radiant pages in the
biography of souls.* David Thomas

❋

It's nice to be important, but it's more important to be nice.
Unknown

❋

*I feel a very unusual sensation—if it is not indigestion, I think it
must be gratitude.* Benjamin Disraeli

✳

I would maintain that thanks are the highest form of thought,
and that gratitude is happiness doubled by wonder.
G K Chesterton

✳

Not what we give,
But what we share,
For the gift
without the giver
is bare.
James Russell Lowell

✳

How far that little candle throws his beams!
So shines a good deed in a weary world.
William Shakespeare

Congratulations on Your ...

NEW HOME

● ●

May every day in your new home create memories that
will be cherished forever.

✳

May God bless your new house as you make it a home.

✳

May the time shared together in your new home be full of love and laughter.

✳

Congratulations on your new home. We're looking forward to spending time with you there.

✳

It's the people in the house that make it a home, so we know yours will be a beautiful one.

✳

Home, the spot of earth supremely blest,
A dearer, sweeter spot than all the rest.
Robert Montgomery

✳

May your home always be too small to hold all of your friends.   Unknown

✳

I am grateful for the lawn that needs mowing, windows that need cleaning, and floors that need waxing because it means I have a home.   Unknown

✳

May your walls know joy;
May every room hold laughter
And every window open to
Great possibility.
Unknown

✳

It takes hands to build a house, but only hearts can build a home.
Unknown

✳

Where we love is home—home that our feet may leave,
but not our hearts.   Oliver Wendell Holmes, Sr

❊

Every house where love abides
And friendship is a guest,
Is surely home, and home sweet home
For there the heart can rest.
Henry Van Dyke

❊

The ornaments of your house will be the guests who frequent it.
Unknown

❊

The fellow that owns his own home is always just coming out
of a hardware store.   Frank McKinney Hubbard

PROMOTION

Congratulations on your promotion. You deserve it.

❊

For someone who works as hard as you, it was only
a matter of time. Well done.

❊

We knew they would see your potential eventually.

❊

It couldn't have happened to a better person. Congratulations.

❊

Accomplishing the impossible means only that the boss
will add it to your regular duties. Doug Larson

By working faithfully eight hours a day you may eventually get to be boss and work twelve hours a day. Robert Frost

✻

Executive ability is deciding quickly and getting somebody else to do the work. John G Pollard

✻

I cannot put into words just how much promotion means to me but if I could I would put it in a can so I could open it later.
Steve Coppell

NEW JOB

Congratulations. May this job be everything you hoped it would be.

✻

Congratulations. You'll do great.

✻

Hoping your new job is so great you won't be able to stop smiling.

✻

Enjoy the journey and remember to have fun.

✻

Congrats. Hoping this new job is the beginning of an even better future.

✻

Find a job you like and you add five days to every week.
H Jackson Browne

✻

The best way to appreciate your job is to imagine yourself without one. Oscar Wilde

✳

*Choose a job you love, and you will never have to work
a day in your life.* Confucius

✳

*Don't waste time learning the 'tricks of the trade'. Instead, learn
the trade.* Attributed to both James Charlton and H Jackson Brown

✳

*The brain is a wonderful organ. It starts working the moment you
get up in the morning, and does not stop until you get into
the office.* Robert Frost

✳

If you have a job without any aggravations, you don't have a job.
Malcolm S Forbes

✳

*The supreme accomplishment is to blur the line
between work and play.* Arnold Toynbee

✳

Many people quit looking for work when they find a job. Unknown

✳

*The difference between a job and a career is the difference
between forty and sixty hours a week.* Robert Frost

✳

*When people go to work, they shouldn't have to leave
their hearts at home.* Betty Bender

✳

*A lot of fellows nowadays have a B.A., M.D., or Ph.D.
Unfortunately, they don't have a J.O.B.* 'Fats' Domino

✳

Time is an illusion, lunchtime doubly so. Douglas Adams

Whenever it is possible, a boy should choose some occupation which he should do even if he did not need the money.
William Lyon Phelps

NEW BUSINESS

A business that makes nothing but money is a poor business.
Henry Ford

❉

All the best with your new business venture.
We know it will be very successful.

❉

You have always succeeded in everything you do.
We know this will be no different ... All the best.

❉

With your enthusiasm and commitment, your new business is guaranteed to succeed.

❉

The sign on the door of opportunity reads PUSH.   Unknown

❉

I'm not a driven businessman, but a driven artist. I never think about money. Beautiful things make money.   Lord Acton

❉

When in doubt, mumble; when in trouble, delegate; when in charge, ponder.   James H Boren

The secret to productive goal setting is in establishing clearly defined goals, writing them down and then focusing on them several times a day with words, pictures and emotions as if we've already achieved them. Denis Waitley

✳

Most of what we call management consists of making it difficult for people to get their work done. Peter Drucker

✳

As a small businessperson, you have no greater leverage than the truth. John Greenleaf Whittier

✳

In the business world, everyone is paid in two coins: cash and experience. Take the experience first; the cash will come later. Harold S Geneen

✳

The secret to managing is to keep the guys who hate you away from the guys who are undecided. Casey Stengel

✳

And while the law of competition may be sometimes hard for the individual, it is best for the race, because it ensures the survival of the fittest in every department. Andrew Carnegie

✳

I rate enthusiasm even above professional skill. Edward Appleton

✳

High achievement always takes place in the framework of high expectation. Charles Kettering

✳

Do more than is required. What is the distance between someone who achieves their goals consistently and those who spend their lives and careers merely following? The extra mile. Gary Ryan Blair

Every young man would do well to remember that all successful business stands on the foundation of morality.
Henry Ward Beecher

❆

Remind people that profit is the difference between revenue and expense. This makes you look smart. Scott Adams

GRADUATION

· ·

Congratulations. Reach for the stars.

❆

We are proud of you (name) ... Your commitment and enthusiasm have been inspiring ... Well done.

❆

When we finish something, it's followed by a new beginning. I'm looking forward to hearing all about yours.

❆

Well done. You've worked hard and deserve a successful and promising future.

❆

Today is the promise of a very bright future. Congratulations.

❆

The world is full of exciting possibilities and they have just been opened up to you. Have fun exploring them.

❆

Con 'grad' ulations!

❆

Your families are extremely proud of you. You can't imagine the sense of relief they are experiencing. This would be a most opportune time to ask for money. Gary Bolding

✴

The important thing is not to stop questioning. Albert Einstein

✴

An investment in knowledge always pays the best interest.
Benjamin Franklin

✴

A graduation ceremony is an event where the commencement speaker tells thousands of students dressed in identical caps and gowns that 'individuality' is the key to success. Robert Orben

✴

The man who graduates today and stops learning tomorrow is uneducated the day after. Newton D Baker

✴

At commencement you wear your square-shaped mortarboards. My hope is that from time to time you will let your minds be bold, and wear sombreros. Paul Freund

Christmas

I will honour Christmas in my heart,
and try to keep it all the year.
Charles Dickens

❊

Christmas is a time for eating, laughing, caring, sharing, giving and receiving. I hope you experience all of them.

❊

May your home be filled with love, laughter and Christmas spirit.

❊

Wishing you joy on this special season of miraculous wonder.

❊

May your Christmas be bright with, love, joy and light.
From our family to yours ... Merry Christmas.

❊

May the beauty of this season fill your heart and home with joy ...
Merry Christmas.

❊

May you look back on this wonderful Christmas season throughout the year with fond memories of fun times.

❊

May the peace of God be with you and your family this holiday season and may He keep you safe from harm ... All our love the (name) Family.

❊

Although the weather is warm, may you be snowed under with love, joy and peace this Christmas.

❊

May your Christmas be a blessed one with family and friends.

✳

A silent night with a bright shining star ... May this Christmas fill you with peace, hope, and joy to sustain you through the New Year.

✳

May each day of this holiday season be full of love, friendship and peace ... Merry Christmas.

✳

As we celebrate the birth of Jesus, I pray this Christmas brings you joy.

✳

Wishing you a beautiful Christmas season with time for relaxation and contemplation.

✳

It's a busy time of year, make sure you find time to stop and enjoy.

✳

As you awake on Christmas morn, lie still a moment and enjoy a moment's peace before the onslaught of children and wrapping paper.

✳

Your Merry Christmas may depend on what others do for you ... but your Happy New Year depends on what you do for others.
Unknown

✳

Love is what's in the room with you at Christmas if you stop opening presents and listen. Unknown

✳

Remember, if Christmas isn't found in your heart, you won't find it under a tree. Charlotte Carpenter

✳

Sugar and Spice makes Christmas Nice! Unknown

❅

Three wonderful little words at Christmas ... No Assembly Required!
Unknown

❅

*One of the most glorious messes in the world is the mess created in
the living room on Christmas day. Don't clean it up too quickly.*
Andy Rooney

❅

*A little smile, a word of cheer,
A bit of love from someone near,
A little gift from one held dear,
Best wishes for the coming year ...
These make a Merry Christmas!*
John Greenleaf Whittier

❅

*Peace on earth will come to stay,
when we live Christmas every day.* Helen Steiner Rice

❅

Christmas cookies and happy hearts, this is how the holiday starts.
Unknown

❅

Perhaps the best Yuletide decoration is being wreathed in smiles.
Unknown

❅

*Christmas waves a magic wand over this world, and behold,
everything is softer and more beautiful.* Norman Vincent Peale

❅

*Bless us Lord, this Christmas, with quietness of mind;
Teach us to be patient and always to be kind.* Helen Steiner Rice

❅

It is Christmas in the heart that puts Christmas in the air.   W T Ellis

✳

For centuries men have kept an appointment with Christmas.
Christmas means fellowship, feasting, giving and receiving,
a time of good cheer, home.   W J Tucker

✳

Christmas is forever, not for just one day,
for loving, sharing, giving, are not to put away
like bells and lights and tinsel, in some box upon a shelf.
The good you do for others is good you do yourself.
Norman W Brooks, *Let Every Day Be Christmas*

✳

At Christmas, all roads lead home.   Marjorie Holmes

✳

Gifts of time and love are surely the basic ingredients for a truly
Merry Christmas.   Peg Bracken

✳

Every time we love, every time we give, it's Christmas.
Dale Evans

✳

There's nothing sadder in this world than to awake Christmas
morning and not be a child.   Erma Bombeck

✳

From a commercial point of view, if Christmas did not exist
it would be necessary to invent it.
Katherine Whitehorn in her book *Roundabout*

✳

Christmas is not a time nor a season, but a state of mind. To
cherish peace and goodwill, to be plenteous in mercy, is to have
the real spirit of Christmas.   Calvin Coolidge

I wish we could put some of the Christmas spirit in jars and open a jar of it every month.
Harlan Miller

✻

Christmas gift suggestions:
To your enemy, forgiveness.
To an opponent, tolerance.
To a friend, your heart.
To a customer, service.
To all, charity.
To every child, a good example.
To yourself, respect.
Oren Arnold

Easter

Jesus took my place on the cross
to give me a place in heaven.   Unknown

✻

Take time to contemplate the miracle of Easter and let this fill your heart with warmth.

✻

Let your faith be renewed this Easter.

✻

Thinking of you and your family this Easter. May it be filled with love laughter and above all ... chocolate.

✻

May your Easter be as warm and fuzzy as the bunny
who delivered your eggs!

❊

May your heart and home be filled with God's blessings this Easter.

❊

As we celebrate this special season let's not forget
God's awesome gift ... Happy Easter.

❊

Let us rejoice today as we remember the death and celebrate the
resurrection of our Lord Jesus Christ. Hallelujah.

❊

Warm hot cross buns with melted butter, chocolate in every shape and
form ... mmm, smells like Easter! ... Have a great day.

❊

*The resurrection gives my life meaning and direction and the
opportunity to start over no matter what my circumstances.*
Robert Flatt

❊

But from this earth, this grave, this dust,
My God shall raise me up, I trust.
Walter Raleigh

❊

Jesus lives, to Him the Throne
Over all the world is given,
May we go where He is gone,
Rest and reign with Him in heaven.
Alleluia!
Christian Furchtegott Gellert

Easter spells out beauty, the rare beauty of new life. S D Gordon

The cross of Christ shows us that God's love is of deepest descent ...
universal distribution and of eternal duration. Dr Fred Barlow

Let the resurrection joy lift us from loneliness and weakness and
despair to strength and beauty and happiness. Floyd W Tomkins

For I remember it is Easter morn,
And life and love and peace are all new born.
Alice Freeman Palmer

Let every man and woman count himself immortal. Let him catch
the revelation of Jesus in his resurrection. Let him say not merely,
'Christ is risen', but 'I shall rise'. Phillips Brooks

Where man sees but withered leaves, God sees sweet flowers
growing. Albert Laighton

We live and die; Christ died and lived! John Stott

Get Well

The greatest healing therapy is friendship and love.
Hubert Humphrey

✻

Hoping each day brings you renewed strength, a brighter smile
and a happier you. Get well soon.

✻

Get well soon but not so quickly that you don't get to enjoy the
benefits of convalescing. Enjoy being cared for. You deserve it.

✻

We miss you and wish you a speedy recovery.
Nothing's the same when you're not here.

✻

Every day is a little better than the day before. Take it easy.

✻

Sending you wishes that each day brings you renewed strength
and a healthier and happier you.

✻

We are all wishing you happy healing and a speedy recovery.

✻

Getting back to health is easy enough ... It's getting back to work
that's tough! Get well soon.

✻

Sending you heartfelt warmth and wishes,
hope you're feeling better soon.

✻

You are always doing so much for everyone else.
Please rest and let everyone wait on you.

✳

I was going to cook you some chicken soup ... then I thought,
wait (he/she) is sick already, leave the cooking to the experts.

✳

Looking forward to having you back on your feet ... it's not the same
without you. Get well soon.

✳

Won't be long and you will be your perky self again ...
enjoy the remote while you can.

✳

Life's no fun without you ... Get well soon.

A kiss makes everything better ... here are two XX ... We miss you.
Get well soon.

✳

Ever feel like the universe is slowing you down?
Slow down and enjoy the pace and let others take care of you.

✳

Heard you were feeling a bit under the weather ...
hope the sun shines soon.

✳

The best six doctors anywhere
And no one can deny it
Are sunshine, water, rest, and air
Exercise and diet.
These six will gladly you attend
If only you are willing
Your mind they'll ease
Your will they'll mend
And charge you not a shilling.
Nursery rhyme quoted by Wayne Fields in *What the River Knows*

✻

*Since you've been sick there's been a vacuum ... and no-one knows
how to run it! Get Well Soon.*   Unknown

✻

*I wonder why you can always read a doctor's bill and
you can never read his prescription.*   Finley Peter Dunne

✻

Sleep, riches, and health to be truly enjoyed must be interrupted.
Johann Paul Friedrich Richter

✻

*There are many reasons for you to get well.
Your family loves and needs you,
your family is worried about you ...
... your family is totally unsupervised in your kitchen.*
Unknown

Sympathy

A human life is a story told by God.
Hans Christian Andersen

✻

We take comfort in knowing (name of deceased) is no longer suffering.
(He/She) will remain in our hearts forever. We send thoughts of
comfort to you in your time of grieving.

✻

(Name of deceased) was a blessing and a gift whose memory will be
cherished forever. Our hearts go out to you in your time of sorrow.

Please accept our condolences. We are thinking of you
at this difficult time.

✻

Remembering you and your family at this difficult time.
Our sincerest sympathy.

✻

Praying you find the strength you need to get through this profound
loss. (Name of deceased) will be sorely missed.

✻

May the memories of your loved one never fade and be a constant
reminder of all that was beautiful in (Name's) time with you.

✻

May you find comfort in knowing (name of deceased) touched the
lives of everyone they met and our lives have been enriched for
having known (him/her).

✻

May the memories of your time together bring you comfort.
(Name of deceased) will live on in all our hearts.

✻

Don't forget God is with you, by your side at this difficult time.
As are we, your friends and family.

✻

(Name of deceased) was a source of inspiration to many.
(He/She) will never be forgotten.

✻

May your heart find peace in the love of your
family and friends at this time.

✻

Please know I am here to help in any way. May your heart
and soul find peace and comfort during this difficult time.

❋

Unable are the loved to die. For love is immortality.
Emily Dickinson

❋

When you are sorrowful look again in your heart, and you shall see that in truth you are weeping for that which has been your delight.
Kahlil Gibran

❋

In the night of death, hope sees a star, and listening love can hear the rustle of a wing. Robert Ingersoll

❋

They that love beyond the world cannot be separated by it. Death cannot kill what never dies. William Penn

❋

Although it's difficult today to see beyond the sorrow,
May looking back in memory help comfort you tomorrow.
Unknown

❋

Death leaves a heartache no-one can heal,
love leaves a memory no-one can steal. On a headstone

❋

Perhaps they are not the stars, but rather openings in Heaven where the love of our lost ones pours through and shines down upon us to let us know they are happy.
Unknown

❋

Life is eternal, and love is immortal,
and death is only a horizon;
and a horizon is nothing save the limit of our sight.

Rossiter Worthington Raymond

The most authentic thing about us is our capacity to create, to overcome, to endure, to transform, to love and to be greater than our suffering. Ben Okri

✻

The season of mourning, like spring, summer, fall and winter, will also pass. Molly Fumia

✻

While we are mourning the loss of our friend, others are rejoicing to meet him behind the veil. John Taylor

Retirement

Don't simply retire from something;
have something to retire to. Harry Emerson Fosdick

✻

Enjoy those Monday morning sleep-ins.
Congratulations on your retirement.

✻

The start of something new, you have earned it. Enjoy!

✻

You have made such a difference in your time here.
You have touched and influenced so many. Thank you.

✻

We will never forget all you have achieved.
Good luck in your retirement.

❋

Look forward to each new day in happy anticipation ...
All the best for your retirement.

❋

You have opened the door to a new beginning. Enjoy!

❋

May this be the start of many new adventures. Congratulations.

❋

You will be so missed. Please come and visit.

❋

May good luck be with you in this new season of your life.

❋

You were the key to our success.
Thank you and good luck in your new life.

❋

I hope one day I will work again with someone as special as you.
All the best.

❋

The challenge of retirement is how to spend time without spending money. Unknown

❋

When a man retires, his wife gets twice the husband but only half the income. Chi Chi Rodriguez

❋

When a man retires and time is no longer a matter of urgent importance, his colleagues generally present him with a watch.
R C Sherriff

❋

When you retire, you switch bosses—from the one who hired you to the one who married you. Gene Perret

❊

The best time to start thinking about your retirement is before the boss does. Unknown

❊

A retired husband is often a wife's full-time job. Ella Harris

❊

Retirement is wonderful. It's doing nothing without worrying about getting caught at it. Gene Perret

❊

The trouble with retirement is that you never get a day off. Abe Lemons

❊

Retirement has been a discovery of beauty for me. I never had the time before to notice the beauty of my grandkids, my wife, the tree outside my very own front door. And, the beauty of time itself. Hartman Jule

❊

The question isn't at what age I want to retire, it's at what income. George Foreman

❊

When men reach their 60s and retire, they go to pieces. Women go right on cooking. Gail Sheehy

❊

I enjoy waking up and not having to go to work. So I do it three or four times a day. Gene Perret

Bon Voyage

A vacation is having nothing to do and all day to do it in.
Robert Orben

We're going to miss you. Have a great trip and spare a thought
for us less fortunate.

Wish I was coming too. Got room in your suitcase?

❉

Bon Voyage! Have an exciting and memorable holiday.

❉

May this holiday be the best one yet.

❉

Don't be gone too long ... we're going to miss you.
Have a great holiday.

❉

*Remember —sometimes the road less travelled is less travelled
for a reason.* Jerry Seinfeld

❉

*Those that say you can't take it with you never saw a car
packed for a vacation trip.* Unknown

❉

A good vacation is over when you begin to yearn for your work.
Morris Fishbein

Apology

An apology is a good way to have the last word.
Unknown

✽

Admitting I am wrong is a hard thing to do, but seeing you hurt is the hardest of all. I'm sorry.

✽

I was wrong. Please forgive me. All I want more than anything is your forgiveness and to kiss and make up.

✽

I'm so sorry for the hurt I have caused. I will have no peace until you forgive me.

✽

Sorry I wasn't there for you when you needed someone to talk to and a shoulder to cry on.

✽

Can you forgive me? I said words I did not mean, but know I mean this ... I am sorry.

✽

I'm sorry for what I've put you through. It must have been so hard for you. I wish I'd been a better friend. I hope this friendship we can mend.

✽

I know you are so understanding. It is your forgiving nature that makes me love you. Thank you for understanding.

✽

Please forgive me for the damage I have done. Just tell me what I need to do to make it up to you. Nothing would be too hard or too much for your love and forgiveness.

✳

I am so sorry. I hope it is not too late.
Please tell me we are not beyond repair.

✳

I was wrong, you were right ... Sorry.

✳

*In some families, 'please' is described as the magic word.
In our house, however, it was 'sorry'.* Margaret Laurence

✳

*Apology is a lovely perfume; it can transform the clumsiest
moment into a gracious gift.* Margaret Lee Runbeck

✳

*For every minute you are angry, you lose sixty seconds
of happiness.* Unknown

✳

*Keep your words soft and tender because tomorrow
you may have to eat them.* Unknown

✳

Never ruin an apology with an excuse. Kimberly Johnson

✳

*Never apologise for showing feeling. When you do so, you
apologise for the truth.* Benjamin Disraeli

✳

*An apology is the super glue of life. It can repair just about
anything.* Lynn Johnston

✳

*Forgiveness does not change the past, but it does enlarge
the future.* Paul Boese

Inspirational Quotes

When you cease to dream, you cease to live.   Malcolm Forbes

✻

If you don't go after what you want, you'll never have it. If you don't ask, the answer is always 'no'. If you don't step forward, you're always in the same place.   Nora Roberts

✻

The ultimate measure of a man is not where he stands in moments of comfort and convenience, but where he stands at times of challenge and controversy.   Martin Luther King, Jr

✻

One can never consent to creep when one feels an impulse to soar.
Helen Keller

✻

We cannot direct the wind but we can adjust the sails.   Unknown

✻

The future belongs to those who believe in the beauty of their dreams.   Eleanor Roosevelt

✻

When you were born, you cried and the world rejoiced. Live your life so that when you die, the world cries and you rejoice.
Cherokee saying

✻

Faith is taking the first step even when you don't see the whole staircase.   Martin Luther King, Jr

✻

Look at a day when you are supremely satisfied at the end. It's not a day when you lounge around doing nothing; it's when you've had everything to do, and you've done it.
Lord Acton

❊

Our greatest GLORY is not in never failing ... but in RISING every time we fall. Confucius

❊

Do not go where the path may lead, go instead where there is no path and leave a trail. Ralph Waldo Emerson

❊

Only he who can see the invisible can do the impossible.
Frank L Gaines

❊

Only those who will risk going too far can possibly find out how far one can go. T S Eliot

❊

Begin with the end in mind. Stephen Covey

❊

Shoot for the moon. Even if you miss, you'll land among the stars.
Les Brown

❊

Most of the important things in the world have been accomplished by people who have kept on trying when there seemed to be no hope at all. Dale Carnegie

Happiness Quotes

Happiness is not a state to arrive at, but a manner of travelling.
Margaret Lee Runbeck

✻

The grand essentials of happiness are: something to do, something to love, and something to hope for. Allan K Chalmers

✻

Nobody really cares if you're miserable, so you might as well be happy. Cynthia Nelms

✻

The happiest moments of my life have been the few which I have passed at home in the bosom of my family. Thomas Jefferson

✻

The foolish man seeks happiness in the distance, the wise grows it under his feet. James Oppenheim

✻

Happiness is never stopping to think if you are. Palmer Sondreal

✻

You need to learn to be happy by nature, because you'll seldom have the chance to be happy by circumstance.
Lavetta Sue Wegman

✻

Love is a condition in which the happiness of another person is essential to your own. Robert Heinlein

✻

Happiness is when what you think, what you say, and what you do are in harmony. Mohandas K Gandhi

✳

Whoever is happy will make others happy, too.   Mark Twain

✳

Success is not the key to happiness. Happiness is the key to success. If you love what you are doing, you will be successful.
Albert Schweitzer

✳

Happiness is having a large, loving, caring, close-knit family in another city.   George Burns

✳

Wherever you go, no matter what the weather, always bring your own sunshine.   Anthony J D'Angelo

✳

When one door of happiness closes, another opens; but often we look so long at the closed door that we do not see the one which has been opened for us.   Helen Keller

✳

Happiness is nothing more than good health and a bad memory.
Albert Schweitzer

✳

Happiness is as a butterfly which, when pursued, is always beyond our grasp, but which if you will sit down quietly, may alight upon you.
Nathaniel Hawthorne

✳

Let us be grateful to people who make us happy; they are the charming gardeners who make our souls blossom.   Marcel Proust

Love Quotes

Anyone can catch your eye, but it takes someone special to catch your heart. Unknown

❄

Love is like playing the piano. First you must learn to play by the rules, then you must forget the rules and play from your heart.
Unknown

❄

To truly love someone is to put their feelings entirely before your own. Anne Marie Cline

❄

All love that has not friendship for its base, is like a mansion built upon the sand. Ella Wheeler Wilcox

❄

I've fallen in love many times ... always with you. Unknown

❄

True loves comes quietly, without banners or flashing lights. If you hear bells, get your ears checked. Erich Segal

❄

If love is blind, why is lingerie so popular? Unknown

❄

A kiss is a lovely trick designed by nature to stop speech when words become superfluous. Ingrid Bergman

❄

I love you like crazy, baby
'Cuz I'd go crazy without you. Pixie Foudre

❄

Time is too slow for those who wait, too swift for those who fear, too long for those who grieve, too short for those who rejoice, but for those who love, time is eternity. Henry Van Dyke

❄

Love is like a violin. The music may stop now and then, but the strings remain forever. Unknown

❄

We love because it's the only true adventure. Nikki Giovanni

❄

Grow old with me! The best is yet to be. Robert Browning

❄

The most important things are the hardest to say, because words diminish them. Stephen King

❄

Are we not like two volumes of one book?
Marceline Desbordes-Valmore

❄

Love is missing someone whenever you're apart, but somehow feeling warm inside because you're close in heart. Kay Knudsen

❄

Anyone can be passionate, but it takes real lovers to be silly.
Rose Franken

❄

Life is the flower for which love is the honey. Victor Hugo

❄

Love doesn't make the world go round, love is what makes the ride worthwhile. Elizabeth Barrett Browning

❄

Love builds bridges where there are none. R H Delaney

❋

Love is a game that two can play and both win.   Eva Gabor

❋

I love thee to the depth and breadth and height my soul can reach.
Elizabeth Barrett Browning

❋

*Attention is the most basic form of love; through it we bless and
are blessed.*   John Tarrant

❋

Love is the master key that opens the gates of happiness.
Oliver Wendell Holmes

❋

Love is the irresistible desire to be irresistibly desired.   Mark Twain

❋

*I love thee — I love thee,
'Tis all that I can say
It is my vision in the night,
My dreaming in the day.*
Thomas Hood

Fun Quotes

To let a fool kiss you is bad ... to let a kiss fool you is worse.
Unknown

❋

*Kids in the back seat cause accidents. Accidents in the back seat
cause ... kids.*   Unknown

❋

Adults are always asking little kids what they want to be when they grow up because they're looking for ideas. Paula Poundstone

✳

Take my advice. I'm not using it. Unknown

✳

If you expect breakfast in bed, go sleep in the kitchen. Unknown

✳

Mirror, mirror on the wall, I've become my mother after all!
Unknown

✳

An archeologist is the best husband any woman can have; the older she gets, the more interested he is in her. Agatha Christie

✳

You can't put a price tag on love, but you can on all its accessories.
Melanie Clark

✳

The Japanese have a word for it. It's Judo — the art of conquering by yielding. The Western equivalent of judo is, 'Yes, dear'.
J P McEvoy

✳

What I'm looking for is a blessing that's not in disguise.
Kitty O'Neill Collins

✳

Few things are more satisfying than seeing your children have teenagers of their own. Doug Larson

✳

Use your health, even to the point of wearing it out.
George Bernard Shaw

Goodbye/Farewell

We're going to miss you. Please don't be a stranger
and visit once in a while.

✳

Sorry to see you leaving. It has been a pleasure having you around.

✳

Goodbye and Good Luck.

✳

Things won't be the same when you're gone. We'll miss you.

✳

You made coming to work more enjoyable. You'll be missed.

✳

Take me with you.

✳

I don't like goodbyes, so I'll just say 'Till we meet again'.

✳

Sorry you are leaving but I am honoured to have known you.
All the best with wherever life takes you.

✳

One of the highlights of my life has been knowing you.
I know this is not the end.

✳

*Don't be dismayed at goodbyes. A farewell is necessary before you
can meet again. And meeting again, after moments or a lifetime, is
certain for those who are friends.*   Richard Bach

✳

Don't cry because it's over. Smile because it happened.
Attributed to Theodor Seuss Geisel

❊

Man's feelings are always purest and most glowing in the hour of meeting and of farewell. Jean Paul Richter

❊

Goodbye to someone we'll always remember ... from the weird bunch you probably can't wait to forget. Unknown

❊

Those to whom we say farewell, are welcomed by others. Unknown

❊

The return makes one love the farewell. Alfred De Musset

❊

Why does it take a minute to say hello and forever to say goodbye?
Unknown

❊

No distance of place or lapse of time can lessen the friendship of those who are thoroughly persuaded of each other's worth.
Robert Southey

❊

A goodbye isn't painful unless you're never going to say hello again. Unknown

❊

A man never knows how to say goodbye; a woman never knows when to say it. Helen Rowland

❊

May the road rise up to meet you, may the wind be ever at your back. May the sun shine warm upon your face and the rain fall softly on your fields. And until we meet again, may God hold you in the hollow of his hand. Irish Blessing